Tiger Sharks

BY LAURA HAMILTON WAXMAN

AMICUS HIGH INTEREST • AMICUS INK

Amicus High Interest and Amicus Ink are imprints of Amicus
P.O. Box 227, Mankato, MN 56002
www.amicuspublishing.us

Library of Congress Cataloging-in-Publication Data
Waxman, Laura Hamilton, author.
Tiger sharks / by Laura Hamilton Waxman.
pages cm. – (Sharks)
Audience: K to grade 3.
Includes bibliographical references and index.
ISBN 978-1-60753-980-3 (library binding)
ISBN 978-1-68152-093-3 (pbk.)
ISBN 978-1-68151-014-9 (ebook)
1. Tiger shark–Juvenile literature. 2. Sharks–Juvenile literature.
I. Title.
QL638.95.C3W39 2017
597.3'4–dc23
2015033752

Editor: Wendy Dieker
Series Designer: Kathleen Petelinsek
Book Designer: Aubrey Harper
Photo Researcher: Rebecca Bernin

Photo Credits: Image Source/Superstock cover; Jim Abernethy/Getty 5; Masa Ushioda/Alamy 6; Bernard Radvaner/Corbis 8–9; Corbis 10; age fotostock/Alamy 13; Sylvain Girardot/Water Rights/Corbis 14; Matt Heath/Alamy 17; ArteSub/Alamy 18; Matt Heath/Alamy 20–21; frantisekhojdysz/Shutterstock 22; Anna Jedynak/Shutterstock 25; Jeffrey Rotman/Corbis 26; Stephen Frink/Getty 29

Table of Contents

Deadly Nighttime Hunter

Night has come. In the dark water swims a deadly hunter. It's a tiger shark. And it's heading toward shore. Quietly, it sneaks up on a sea turtle. Then it opens its huge jaws. Crunch! The tiger shark's powerful teeth bust through the turtle's shell. It has caught its first meal of the night.

A tiger shark shows off rows of sharp teeth strong enough to crack a sea turtle's shell.

A striped tiger shark swims above a lemon shark in shallow ocean waters.

Q How did tiger sharks get their name?

Tiger sharks are one of the world's largest sharks. Most tiger sharks are about 10 to 14 feet (3 to 4 m) long. But some grow up to 25 feet (7.5 m). Their skin color matches the ocean around them. Some tiger sharks are blue-green on top. Others are dark gray. They are yellow or white on the bottom.

A Young tiger sharks are born with dark stripes. The stripes look like tiger stripes. They fade as the sharks grow up.

A tiger shark has eight **fins**. The fins are stiff and strong. The tiger shark uses them to swim. Two fins are on its back. They help keep the shark steady. Two fins look like wings on a plane. They help the shark steer. Three fins under the shark's body help it change directions. And a tail fin pushes the shark forward.

This shark's eight fins move it through the water.

A shark's snout senses the movements made by other creatures in the water.

A tiger shark has a wide, flat **snout**. On its snout are nostrils for smelling. The snout also has special sensors. These can feel electricity in the water. When animals move, they give off tiny electric waves. A tiger shark can feel that. It also has **gills**. The gills allow it to breathe underwater.

Catching Dinner

Tiger sharks are **carnivores**. They hunt and eat other animals. Sea turtles, fish, and squid are food for tiger sharks. So are shellfish, sea birds, and other sharks. Tiger sharks even eat dead whales. And that's not all. Tiger sharks eat trash floating in the water. They've eaten cans, bottles, tires, and many other things.

Q Why do tiger sharks eat trash?

A passing squid could soon become part of a hungry tiger shark's meal.

A Tiger sharks are not picky eaters. And their sharp teeth can bite into almost anything. Some people even call them "trash cans of the sea."

This tiger shark snatches up whole fish. And that's only a snack!

Tiger sharks mostly hunt at night. They swim close to shore when darkness falls. There they slowly search for **prey**. Their eyes are made to see at night. They speed up when prey is near. Then their jaws open wide. Chomp! They bite down on the prey. Their teeth cut right through. Crunch! They eat through bone and shell.

Having Babies

Tiger sharks live alone. But they pair up in spring to **mate**. After that, new sharks start to grow in the female. These new sharks are inside eggs. The new sharks grow for up to 16 months. Then they hatch inside their mother. The mother gives birth to her **pups** and swims away.

Q How many tiger shark pups are born at a time?

Tiger sharks come together to mate in the spring.

A tiger shark mother gives birth to 10 to 80 pups.

The marks on this tiger shark pup are still quite dark. They help it blend into the shadows.

Q How long do tiger sharks live?

Baby tiger sharks are called pups. The pups are much smaller than their mother. They are tasty treats for other sharks. But tiger shark pups can hide from **predators**. Their black stripes blend in with the shadows, so they're harder to find. They're also fast swimmers. They can race from danger.

A Tiger sharks often live for about 25 years. But some live for up to 50 years.

Tiger shark pups must find enough food to eat. Luckily, they are born knowing how to hunt. The pups hunt fish and other small animals. They grow bigger and bigger each year. Their stripes fade more and more. Tiger shark pups are all grown up after 6 to 8 years.

A tiny newborn pup is next to its mother. But not for long.

Tiger sharks eat almost anything, but they don't bother divers taking photos.

Staying Alive in the Ocean

Tiger sharks are big and tough. That makes them **apex predators**. Apex predators are at the top of the food chain. No other animals hunt them. Even so, tiger sharks face dangers. The biggest danger is hunger. Tiger sharks need a lot of food to survive. Eating many kinds of sea animals helps. Tiger sharks don't run out of food easily.

Tiger sharks must also stay in water that is safe. Tiger sharks are **cold-blooded**. Their body temperature matches the water temperature. The water gets too cold for tiger sharks in winter. So they must **migrate** to warmer waters. That warm water gets too hot in summer. So they travel back to cooler waters.

Tiger sharks swim to warm places like this in the winter.

Some people capture tiger sharks that get too close to swimming beaches.

Q How often do tiger sharks attack people?

Tiger Sharks and People

People are another big danger to tiger sharks. Some people hunt tiger sharks to eat. Other people hunt tiger sharks out of fear. Sometimes a tiger shark thinks a human is prey. Then it attacks. Often, the person dies. Some people kill tiger sharks to keep them away.

A

Tiger sharks attack more often than other sharks. Even so, fewer than 80 attacks happen worldwide each year. And not all of those attacks are by tiger sharks.

Most tiger sharks don't attack people. And most people don't hunt tiger sharks. But there are now fewer tiger sharks in the world. People are working to protect these sharks. They want to keep them safe. Small steps now will mean that tiger sharks can continue to live in our oceans for years to come.

A diver takes pictures of a tiger shark in the warm water.

Glossary

apex predator An animal that hunts large animals and has no predators.

carnivore An animal that hunts and eats other animals.

cold-blooded An animal whose body temperature matches the water or air around it.

fins Body parts that help a fish swim.

gills Body parts an animal uses to breathe underwater.

mate To come together to make babies.

migrate To travel a long distance from one place to another.

predator An animal that hunts other animals.

prey Animals that are hunted by other animals.

pup Baby shark.

snout The nose and mouth of an animal.

Read More

Bell, Samantha. *Tiger Sharks.* Ann Arbor, MI: Cherry Lake Publishing, 2014.

Kratt, Martin and Chris Kratt. *Wild Sea Creatures: Sharks, Whales, and Dolphins!* New York: Random House, 2014.

Reynolds, Shaye. *In Search of Tiger Sharks.* New York: PowerKids Press, 2016.

Websites

Shark Academy
www.oceanicresearch.org

Tiger Sharks | National Geographic
animals.nationalgeographic.com/animals/fish/tiger-shark/

Tiger Shark Videos
www.discovery.com/tv-shows/shark-week/videos/tiger-shark-videos/

Every effort has been made to ensure that these websites are appropriate for children. However, because of the nature of the Internet, it is impossible to guarantee that these sites will remain active indefinitely or that their contents will not be altered.

Index

About the Author

Laura Hamilton Waxman has written and edited many nonfiction books for children. She loves learning about new things—like sharks—and sharing what she's learned with her readers. She lives in St. Paul, Minnesota.